S0-AQL-722

BLOOMINGTON
PUBLIC LIBRARY

DEC 1 0

Cinco de Mayo

Rebecca Rissman

Heinemann Library
Chicago, Illinois

www.heinemannraintree.com
Visit our website to find out more information about Heinemann-Raintree books.

To order:

☎ Phone 888-454-2279

▭ Visit www.heinemannraintree.com to browse our catalog and order online.

©2011 Heinemann Library
an imprint of Capstone Global Library, LLC
Chicago, Illinois

All rights reserved. No part of this publication may be reproduced or transmitted in any form or by any means, electronic or mechanical, including photocopying, recording, taping, or any information storage and retrieval system, without permission in writing from the publisher.

Edited by Adrian Vigliano and Rebecca Rissman
Designed by Ryan Frieson
Picture research by Tracy Cummins
Leveling by Nancy E. Harris
Originated by Capstone Global Library Ltd.
Printed in China by South China Printing Company Ltd.

15 14 13 12 11 10
10 9 8 7 6 5 4 3 2 1

Library of Congress Cataloging-in-Publication Data
Rissman, Rebecca.
   Cinco de Mayo / Rebecca Rissman.
     p. cm.—(Holidays and festivals)
   Includes bibliographical references and index.
   ISBN 978-1-4329-4059-1 (hc)—ISBN 978-1-4329-4078-2 (pb) 1. Cinco de Mayo (Mexican holiday)—Juvenile literature. 2. Cinco de Mayo, Battle of, Puebla, Mexico, 1862—Juvenile literature. I. Title.
   F1233.R57 2011
   394.262—dc22   2009052861

Acknowledgments

The author and publishers are grateful to the following for permission to reproduce copyright material: AP Photo/The Daily Times, Dave Watson **p.18**; AP Photo/Peter M. Fredin **p.20**; Corbis ©YURI GRIPAS/Reuters **p.5**; Corbis ©Charles & Josette Lenars **p.15**; Corbis ©Keith Dannemiller **p.19**; Getty Images/ColorBlind Images **p.4**; Getty Images/Time & Life Pictures **p.6**; Getty Images/Apic **pp.10, 23 bottom**; Getty Images/Joe Raedle **pp.17, 23 center**; istockphoto ©Aldo Murillo **p.21**; istockphoto ©Leo Blanchette **p.22**; Library of Congress Prints and Photographs Division **pp.7, 23 top**; Shutterstock/trubach **p.8 bottom**; Shutterstock/c. **p.8 center**; Shutterstock/yui **p.8 top**; Shutterstock/Travel Bug **p.16**; The Bridgeman Art Library International/Felix Francois Barthelemy (1826-80)/Museo Centrale del Risorgimento, Rome, Italy **p.9**; The Bridgeman Art Library International/Look and Learn **p.11**; The Bridgeman Art Library International/Archives Charmet **p.13**; The Bridgeman Art Library International/Museo Nacional de Historia, Castillo de Chapultepec, Mexico **p.14**; The Granger Collection, New York **p.12**.

Cover photograph of festival dancers in Mexico reproduced with permission of Getty Images/Larry Dale Gordon. Back cover photograph reproduced with permission of Shutterstock/Travel Bug.

Every effort has been made to contact copyright holders of any material reproduced in this book. Any omissions will be rectified in subsequent printings if notice is given to the publisher.

Contents

What Is a Holiday? 4

The Story of Cinco de Mayo. . . .6

Celebrating
Cinco de Mayo. 16

Cinco de Mayo Symbols 20

Calendar. 22

Picture Glossary 23

Index 24

What Is a Holiday?

A holiday is a special day.
People celebrate holidays.

Cinco de Mayo is a holiday.
Cinco de Mayo is Spanish for May 5.

The Story of Cinco de Mayo

In the 1800s, Mexico was a new country. Benito Juarez was the president.

Mexico fought in many battles to become free. These battles cost a lot of money.

Mexico had borrowed money from Spain, France, and the United States.

Napoleon III was the ruler of France. He wanted money from Mexico. He wanted to take land from Mexico.

9

The French army was well trained.
They had good weapons.

The Mexican army was not well trained.
Their weapons were old.

In 1861 French soldiers attacked
Mexico. The French army came to a
12 city called Puebla to fight.

The Mexican army fought hard.

The French army could not beat the Mexican army.

Mexico won the Battle of Puebla on May 5, 1862.

Celebrating Cinco de Mayo

On Cinco de Mayo people listen to music.

People watch parades.

People wear special clothes and dance.

On Cinco de Mayo people remember
Mexico's victory over France.

Cinco de Mayo Symbols

The Mexican flag is a symbol of Cinco de Mayo.

It reminds Mexican people to be grateful for their country.

Calendar

Cinco de Mayo is on May 5th.

Picture Glossary

 **battle** a large fight between two or more groups of people

 **parade** group of people marching together to celebrate something

 **weapon** an object used during a fight to hurt someone

Index

battle 7, 15, 23

clothes 18

flag 20

music 16

parades 17, 23

president 6

weapons 10, 11, 23

Note to Parents and Teachers

Before reading

Show children a map of North America pointing out Mexico. Explain that every May 5th, Mexicans and many Mexican-Americans celebrate Cinco de Mayo. Are the children familiar with the holiday? What are their impressions? Perhaps they have direct experience with the holiday?

After reading

Throw a Cinco de Mayo fiesta. Have children make and decorate the room with paper flowers and Mexican flags. Bring in a variety of Mexican food and music. For extra fun, purchase or make a piñata.